A METHOD FOR DIATONIC HARMONICA
By DAVID McKELVY

The audio coordinates with the book, reinforcing many of the music elements you'll learn about, and also provides the melody and background tracks for many of the songs. A symbol ◆ like this appears as a signal that the material is on the recording.

DAVID McKELVY

David McKelvy is known in the music industry as one of the best and most versatile players of the harmonica. His styles range from blues and country, to rock and to classical. As a recording musician he has worked in motion pictures, television, commercials and recordings.

Composers and arrangers with whom David has worked include Henry Mancini, the late Nelson Riddle, Arthur Rubinstein, John Barry, Van Dyke Parks and David Rose. David has also been seen and heard on stage in *Shenandoah, Our Town* and *A Lie Of The Mind*.

Flip on the TV and you'll hear David on a multitude of television programs and feature films including *Honky Tonk Man, Any Which Way You Can, Barbarosa, Tour Of Duty, Smokey And The Bandit, Part 2, Cheers, Newhart,* and *Thirtysomething*.

Based in Los Angeles, David performs extensively in clubs and concerts, and also teaches harmonica privately and in groups that include college workshops.

Edited by Ronny S. Schiff
Harmonica Design by Elyse Morris Wyman & Ralf Eichert
Book Graphic Design by Elyse Morris Wyman & Ronny Schiff
Cartoons by Anita McLaughlin & Sally Rosenberg
Diagrams by Ralf Eichert & Keith McMurtrie
With special thanks to Kendall

HAL•LEONARD®
CORPORATION
7777 W. BLUEMOUND RD. P.O. BOX 13819 MILWAUKEE, WI 53213

INTRODUCTION

The purpose of this book is to enable you to become a well-rounded player of the ten-hole diatonic harmonica. Whether your aim is to play blues, country or traditional music, or to become the harmonica's next rock star, you'll have the knowledge to achieve your goal.

As you learn the musical examples and songs, you will realize that this small, fragile instrument you are holding is amazing in its versatility and power of expression. It simply sounds great in a variety of music styles that include blues, country, rock, traditional music and jazz.

Most importantly, with practice and careful listening to your own playing as well as that of others, you can play your harmonica in *your* style. The approach in this book is easy and gradual. The songs are given in standard notation as well as harmonica tablature, so that the method can be used in a classroom situation and taught like other instruments.

Have fun with this book! Read the text straight through or skip around; either way you'll be surprised at the speed with which you learn new songs, keys, and styles.

Enough said, time to play!

CONTENTS

TAKING CARE OF
YOUR HARMONICA

Here are some steps for you to follow so that your harps perform better and last longer:

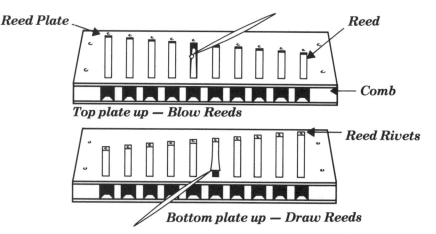

Cover Plate

Screws or Pins

Comb

- Keep your harp away from extremely hot or cold conditions. Extreme temperature conditions can warp both the body and reeds.

- Always place your harp in its container when you are through playing. This will protect it from atmospheric moisture.

- When you finish playing, tap your harp in the palm of your hand to remove the moisture accumulated while blowing.

If a reed sticks and cannot be played after gentle blowing, remove the pins or screws (depending on the model of harmonica). Then locate the reed that is sticking. Place a thin object, such as a toothpick, between the reed and reed plate. You may be able to see the object blocking the reed, or it may be necessary to rub the surfaces where the reed and reed plate meet.

Reed Plate

Reed

Comb

Top plate up — Blow Reeds

Reed Rivets

Bottom plate up — Draw Reeds

At times you may notice that one reed is noticeably closer to, or farther away from, the reed plate. That reed needs to be *regapped* by using a toothpick to pry the reed *(gently)* until its distance from the plate conforms to that of the other reeds. Reeds that are "gapped" too widely from the plate tend to sound windy and lack volume. Reeds "gapped" too close together are either slow to respond or don't play at all.

Manufacturers' warranties against defective harmonicas should be taken seriously. Never accept a harmonica that doesn't play well. Return it to the place of purchase or send it back to the manufacturer for repair or replacement. You will eventually get satisfaction and have a harmonica that will play as well as you.

PART I: LEARNING THE BASICS

You are about to learn the fundamentals of playing harmonica — from producing single notes to playing well-known melodies. Plus, you'll acquire basic music skills that will help you play songs of your own choosing. These skills include understanding rhythms, recognizing keys and reading melodies that are written in both harmonica tablature and standard musical notation.

These skills are uncomplicated to learn if you read the instructions carefully and practice slowly. Play for smoothness, relax and have fun.

Getting Started

To get started, you need the right harmonica, or "harp"(*harp* — the common slang term for harmonica). Your first harmonica should be a good 10-hole *diatonic* harmonica in the key of C. Eventually you may want to buy harps in other keys, but your C-harp will be all that is really necessary in order to learn the songs in this book. The salesperson at your local music store can help you with your choice.

Breathing

People often ask, "Don't you play the harp by blowing out and sucking in?" The answer is: *Sort of, but not exactly.*

In fact, the process of producing notes on your harmonica should be thought of as *INHALING* and *EXHALING,* just as in daily breathing. Breathing too heavily at first will cause notes to sound harsh, muted, or out of tune.

As you breathe, place your right hand across your upper chest and shoulders to be sure they aren't moving up when you inhale. Then, feel your stomach to make sure it *is* expanding. If it is, you are breathing in the most relaxed way possible. Occasionally, while you're playing your harmonica, you should repeat this procedure.

Air goes here.

Holding The Harp

Starting out, hold your harp as shown in this illustration. This will make everything that follows a lot easier.

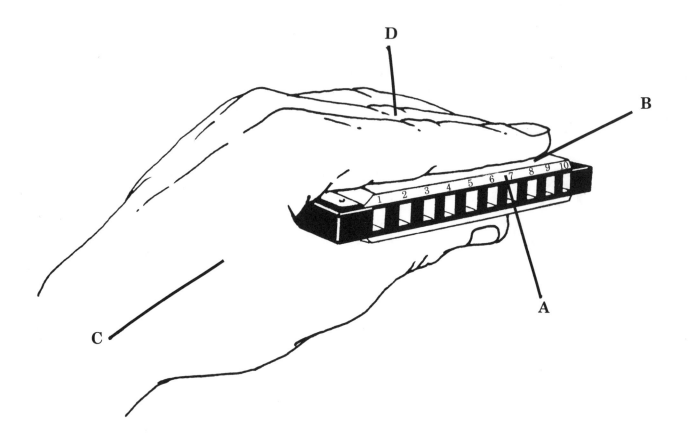

Notice in the diagram...

    A. The hole numbers are on top.

    B. Enough of the mouthpiece protrudes from your thumb and index finger to allow your mouth to fit comfortably over several holes.

    C. The harmonica is held in your left hand *whether you are right or left handed.* (Remember that! There is a reason for it.)

    D. Your remaining three fingers are in a semi-relaxed position, not too stiff, but not completely curled. This position will work best for you when you begin cupping your hands for effects, such as a hand vibrato.

Important Note: As you progress, periodically review these steps.

 # Blowing Your First Single Note

This is a simple but *very important* point in harmonica playing: By learning to blow single notes, you will be able to play recognizable melodies quickly. If the methods you're about to learn seem a little awkward at first, don't worry, the technique is a lot easier than you imagine.

Tongue Blocking

There are two common ways of producing a single note on the harmonica — *lipping* and *tongue blocking.* You should learn both in order to get the widest variety of sounds and rhythms. If you've never played a single note on a harmonica, it's best to learn tongue blocking first.

Here's how tongue blocking works:

- Hold the harmonica in your left hand as shown on page 6.

- Open your mouth in a relaxed manner (without any tension in your jaw muscles) and place the lower-numbered holes in your mouth.

- At this point, don't worry about covering a *specific* number of holes with your lips. If you simply relax your jaw muscles and open your mouth so that the harmonica fits comfortably, you're on the right track. This is important; relaxation is the key to good tone.

- With your mouth in this relaxed position, begin breathing *in* and *out* in a relaxed manner. You should hear groups of at least three notes for each breath. If you hear fewer than three notes or your mouth feels tense, drop your jaw, relax, and place the harmonica in your mouth again until you hear a full group of notes.

- When your breathing produces groups of notes all coming out with equal clarity, place your tongue down *gently* on all the holes except the hole to the *right.* The hole you'll get will be either 3, 4, or 5.

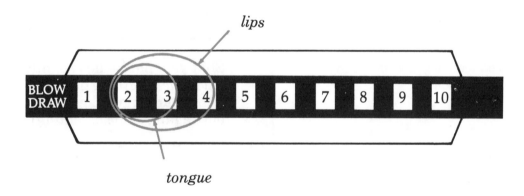

- Continue breathing in and out gently. If you don't hear any sound (or find yourself making raspberry noises through your harp), shift your tongue slightly to the left. Once again, stay relaxed. Just as in speaking and singing, relaxation is the key to sounding good when playing harmonica.

The first time you get a single note in the middle of your harp, hold the note as long as you can. And, even if your next try produces more than one note, remember that having played a single note once, you can do it again! With a little more practice and review of the *Problem/Solution* table on the following page, you will find yourself able to produce single notes almost anywhere on your harmonica.

Here's a table of solutions to problems that may occur when trying to produce single notes. Sometimes there is more than one possible solution, but always try the first solution before the second.

PROBLEM	SOLUTION
No note is produced.	• Shift your tongue very slightly to the left.
More than one note is heard from the right side of your mouth.	• Shift your harmonica very slightly to the left, or... • Shift your tongue slightly to the right.
A single note is heard from the bottom (left side) holes rather than the top (right side) holes.	• Shift your tongue slightly to the left.
Notes are heard from both the right and left sides of your mouth.	• Shift your tongue slightly to the left, or... • Press your tongue lightly on the holes and shift the harmonica to the right.
The note produced is weak and tinny sounding or muted.	• Shift your harmonica slightly to the left *while breathing* or... • Shift your tongue slightly to the left, once again, *while breathing.*
A single note is heard when breathing out, but two notes are heard when breathing in.	• Check to be sure you are not lifting your tongue when breathing in.

As the table indicates, moving your harmonica very slightly in a horizontal motion will usually make the difference between two faint tones and one clear one. Try this before moving your tongue!

Keep breathing in and out producing notes up and down the harmonica. Enjoy the sound! You are now ready to play your first melodies.

Playing A Melody

With practice, producing single notes will seem easier every day.

Tablature

In *harmonica tablature* each note is represented by the number of the hole you are to play...

- Followed by an arrow pointing up (↑) to indicate a *blow* (exhaled) *note*...
- Or an arrow pointing down (↓) to indicate a *draw* (inhaled) *note*.

Here are the melody notes and how they are shown in tablature:

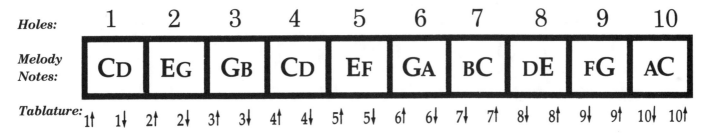

Holes:	1	2	3	4	5	6	7	8	9	10
Melody Notes:	CD	EG	GB	CD	EF	GA	BC	DE	FG	AC
Tablature:	1↑ 1↓	2↑ 2↓	3↑ 3↓	4↑ 4↓	5↑ 5↓	6↑ 6↓	7↓ 7↑	8↓ 8↑	9↓ 9↑	10↓ 10↑

Making Note(s) of Numbers And Arrows

In preparation for your first melody, play this pattern in tablature:

C D E G	A C A G	C E G E	D E C
4↑ 4↓ 5↑ 6↑	6↓ 7↑ 6↓ 6↑	4↑ 5↑ 6↑ 5↑	4↓ 5↑ 4↑

If you are unsure of whether or not you are playing the correct notes, try this:

- Place your index fingers over the holes to the left and right of the hole you are trying to play.
- Listen to yourself playing this note several times and then...
- Find the same note using the tongue blocking technique. Gradually you will acquire a feel for the location of each note, and you will no longer have to search for your notes.

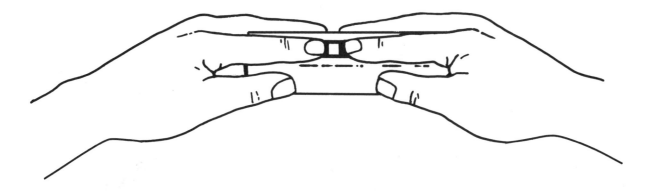

Your First Tune

Enough technical stuff. Here's your first melody which you'll learn just a few notes at a time. "What melody?" you ask! Just play for now, and you'll find out shortly.

- Find hole 6, play the blow note 6↑ three times. Play these notes smoothly but separately.
- On hole 5 play the blow note 5↑ once, and then play 6↑ blow again.
- On hole 6, play the draw note on 6↓ and then play 6↑ blow and 5↑ blow without a break between notes.

(In order to help you become accustomed to reading tablature, only numbers and arrows will be used to teach you the remainder of this melody.)

- Play 5↑ and 4↓, holding the latter note a bit longer.
- Play 5↑ and 4↓ again.

Now practice the sequence of notes you've learned, slowly at first, until you are able to play them together without a break.

You may have recognized that the melody you are learning is *"Camptown Races."* (Surprise!)

By successfully learning this first phase, without knowing in advance what melody you were to play, you can see how easy it is to learn even unfamiliar melodies with the tablature system.

Here's the tablature for *"Camptown Races"* in its entirety:

```
         6↑|  6↑   6↑   5↑   6↑   6↓|  6↑   5↑   | 5↑   4↓          | 5↑   4↓        6↑|
 6↑   6↑   5↑   6↑ |  6↓   6↑   5↑   5↑ |  4↓        5↑   4↓|  4↑              |
 4↑   4↑   5↑   6↑ |  7↑              | 6↓   6↓   7↑   6↓|  6↑                    6↑ |
 6↑   6↑   5↑   6↑ |  6↓   6↑   5↑    | 4↓        5↑   4↓  |  4↑
```

Practice *"Camptown Races"* slowly at first, a few notes at a time (even if it's familiar to you). Make sure that your draw notes are as clear and distinct as your blow notes.

The tablature system is sufficient for learning *"Camptown Races,"* since the song is familiar to most of us. In order to learn less familiar melodies, however, it will help you to look at and learn the following examples of basic music fundamentals. In particular, you will find the information about the length of notes, for example ○ = 4 beats. This is useful for *counting* your songs correctly, even if you choose to rely on tablature for learning the pitches of the notes.

The Basics of Music

• *Staff*

A staff consists of five lines and four spaces. Notes fall on a line or in a space in the staff, or on lines and spaces above or below the staff. These are known as *ledger lines*.

• *Treble Clef*

The treble or G clef occurs at the beginning of each line of music. Note how the loop of the clef circles the G line.

Here are how the melody notes of your harmonica correspond to notes on the staff:

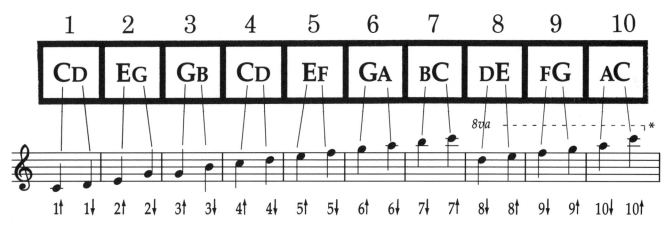

*The *8va sign* above the staff indicates that these notes are to be played one octave — 8 scale notes — higher than written in music notation.

• *Bar Lines*

The staff is divided into sections by *bar lines*. Each section is called a *measure*. A *double bar line* appears at the end of a song:

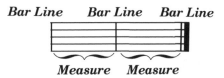

• *Time Signatures*

The top number indicates the number of beats in each measure; the bottom number indicates the type of note that receives one beat:

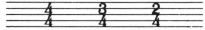

• *Note Values*

Each type of note has a specific *note value* which is measured in rhythmic beats:

Whole Note *4 beats* o	*Half Note* *2 beats* ♩	*Quarter Note* *1 beat* ♩ ♩

Dotted Half Note *3 beats* ♩.	*A dot following a note increases the note length by one half.*

Your First Notes

Whether you choose to rely on harmonica tablature or music notation for learning melodies, it is helpful to learn the names of the notes you are playing.
In *"Camptown Races"* the notes are as follows:

- The first three notes are all G:

- At the end of the second line you are introduced to C:

- The next new notes that you play are E, A and D:

- In the third line, you play only one new note, which is also a C (but higher):

"Camptown Races" with both standard musical notation and harmonica tablature appears below. This song is in 4/4 time (4 beats per measure).

② Camptown Races

Stephen Foster

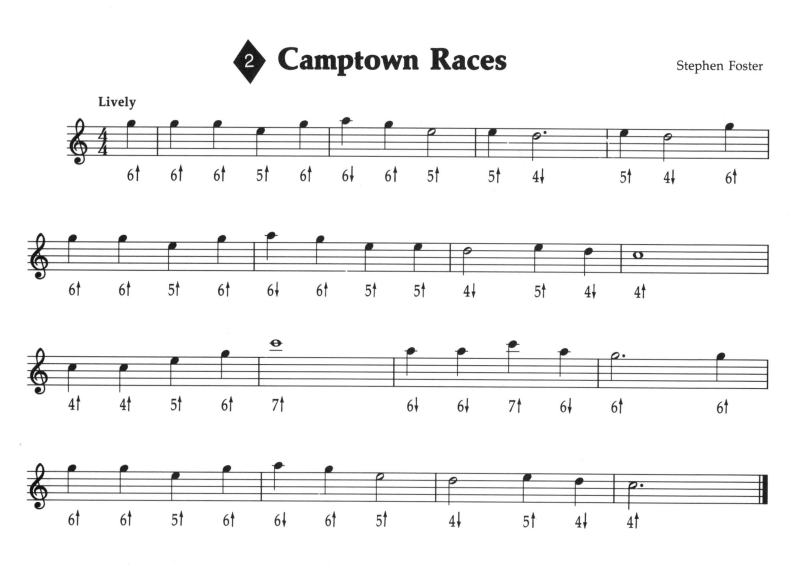

As mentioned before, you should learn the names of the notes on your harmonica whether you choose to read tablature or notation.

More Music (Finally)

The version of *"Camptown Races"* that you learned in *Playing a Melody* is in the key of C major. In order to make learning your next melodies in this key a little easier, here's a basic C scale and a few exercises. The asterisks denote two new notes, F/5↓ and B/7↓:

③ C Scale-From C To Shining C

A scale is the set of notes that define the key in which you are playing. Beginning with the C scale, all musical examples in this book are presented in both tablature and standard music notation. If you wish to learn the tunes from tablature, that's okay. But, if you want to learn to read notation, then it will help you to look at the notes on the staff as you practice these scales, even if you memorize them first from the tablature.

First, practice the ascending and descending scales. Then practice the continuous scale repeatedly without stopping at 7↑ when ascending. Practice for smoothness until there are no audible pauses when you move from one hole to the next, or from a blow note to a draw note.

Pay particular attention to holes 6 and 7 where the blow-draw pattern is reversed. It's very important to get used to this pattern, and it will make learning the next melodies easier.

In the following exercise, play consecutive blow notes (4↑ 5↑) with a single breath. The same applies to consecutive draw notes (4↓ 5↓). Practicing this way will gradually give your playing greater smoothness.

Two new notes are introduced in this exercise:

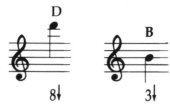

◆4 Skip A Note Scale

"Skip-A-Note Scale" has four beats to each measure. When you practice it in its entirety, start by tapping your foot once for each quarter note and twice for each half note.

Ties

"When The Saints Go Marching In" introduces *ties*:

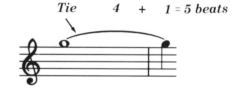

A tie combines *two or more notes of the same pitch*, so that they sound as a single note.

Practice this song slowly at first, then gradually increase your tempo. Listen to yourself as you play. Make sure all your notes sound equally clear.

As you play, your harmonica should slide comfortably in your mouth at a parallel angle, as illustrated on page 6; this angle should never vary.

Count-Off/Pick-ups

You'll notice that this song begins with only three quarter notes prior to the first full measure. This is an example of *pick-up notes*. Many of the musical examples you'll play begin this way — with a note(s) instead of a full measure. A pick-up is counted and played in tempo. Here is an example of a *count-off*:

A count-off establishes the tempo of the song before the first note is played. Learning to start songs with a count-off is important, and is helpful when you play with other musicians.

⬥5 When The Saints Go Marching In

Briskly

Traditional

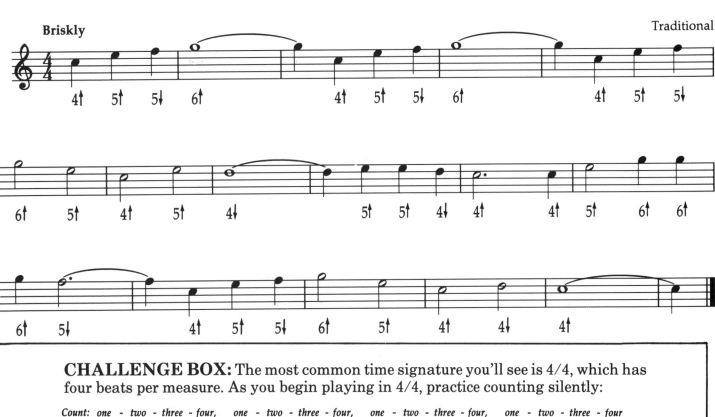

"*Largo*" is your first melody that uses *three/four* time (waltz tempo). As you practice this tune, tap your foot three times each measure, making sure that the first beat is always the strongest.

When you see two dotted half notes joined by a tie, the note you play is six beats long:

⬥6 Largo

Anton Dvorak

Slowly

Once you've learned all the notes, practice for smoothness so that the measures sound connected into a whole melody.

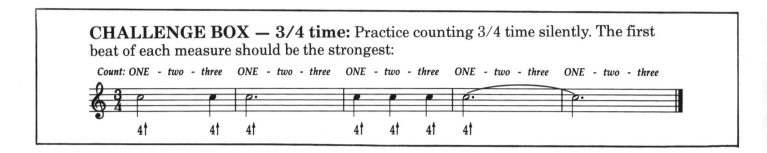

Like "*Largo*," "*Sweet Betsy From Pike*" is also written in 3/4 time. The tempo is fairly quick.

Sweet Betsy From Pike

American Traditional

"*Three And A Third Warm-up*" is good practice for playing the notes that are *consecutive* and those that are *two notes apart*.

Three And A Third Warm-up

There aren't any new musical elements in *"Ode To Joy."* Have fun playing this new tune.

Ode To Joy

Fairly brisk

Ludwig Van Beethoven

Once in a while it's a good idea to review the section about breathing in *Getting Started*.

Ties, Quarters And Eighths

On the next few pages, you'll find examples of rhythms commonly found in every kind of music. Whether you are learning your notes from standard notation or tablature, these exercises and melodies should be practiced until the rhythms are comfortable to play.

Learn the notes of these examples first, practice the rhythms next, and finally practice the melodies in rhythm. All of the examples have simple melodies so that you can focus on their rhythms.

Eighth Notes

You are introduced to eighth notes in *"Au Claire De La Lune."*

- One eighth note equals one-half of a quarter note: ♪ = ½ beat
- Two eighth notes equal one quarter note: ♫ = ♩ 1 beat

Individual eight notes have a single flag and groups of eighth notes are connected by a single beam:

Flag   *Beam*

Practice eighth notes by counting the *number* of the beat as you *tap* your foot and saying "and" as you *lift* your foot:

FOOT: tap.......lift........tap........lift........tap........lift........tap.......lift
COUNT: one.......and........two.......and.......three....and.......four......and

Obviously, you'll count silently when you are playing the melodies, but it will be helpful to you to count them out loud beforehand.

7 Au Claire De La Lune

A Quarter To Eight

This tune mixes quarter notes and eighth notes even more.

Here's a new note:

18

The following tune is simple but useful for practicing tied notes:

Ties And Quarters

David McKelvy

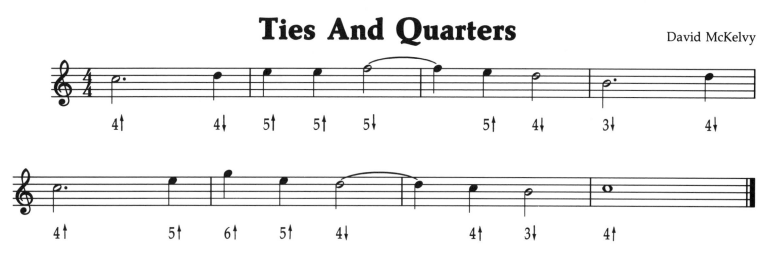

Here are some more examples of ties:

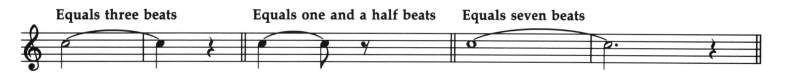

Dotted Quarter Note

As you already learned, the dotted half note receives three beats. A dot placed after a note receives half the value of that note:

$$\text{♩.} = 3 \text{ beats}$$

2 + 1

When the same principle is applied to the dotted quarter note, you have the following:

$$\text{♩.} = 1\frac{1}{2} \text{ beats}$$

1 + ½

Dots, Ties and Eighths

In *"America,"* dotted quarter notes and quarter notes tied to eighth notes are used alternately in order to help you get used to these rhythmic figures and playing the next tunes.

America (My Country 'Tis Of Thee)

American Anthem

◆8 Banks Of The Ohio

American Traditional

If you have any problems with single notes in any passages of the melodies, review the illustrations and table in *Getting Started* that cover holding your harmonica and getting single notes comfortably.

Playing the melodies will gradually become easier, and learning new ones will be a quicker and smoother process. Practice hard, but have fun!

Playing Pretty

As you review and practice the instructions on breathing, relaxation and single note production, what you will hear are increasingly clear, open-sounding notes. Now that your melodies sound cleaner, you can begin to focus on the *sound* you are producing.

When you listen to the music you are playing, you will notice that the tone production process includes more than just your harmonica — the inside of your mouth is acting as a resonating chamber for the notes you are playing.

The first use of your *right hand* will be to create a clean-sounding *vibrato* ("vibrato" — a vibrating effect that varies the pitch of a note; this sound adds color to your playing and gives the longer notes a feeling of motion).

Right Hand Vibrato

There are many varieties of hand vibrato; the easiest position is illustrated here, using the hand position you learned in *Getting Started:*

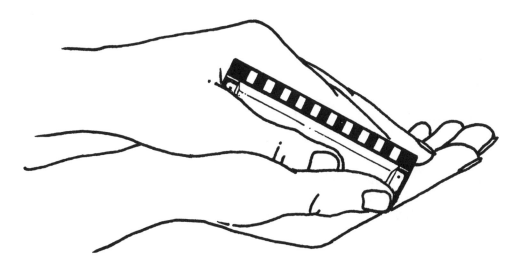

In the illustration, you'll notice that…

• Your left hand position is exactly the same as it has been up to this point (with your fingers curled in a semi-relaxed position).
• Your right hand meets your left hand with your left palm touching your right wrist.

• The fingers of your right hand are curled in a semi-relaxed position, just as those of your left hand.
• The fingertips of your left hand touch the top joints of the fingers of your right hand.
• The blades of your hands are flush with one another, but remain *relaxed.*

The right-hand vibrato is useful in playing traditional music, as well as country and country blues. Learning this method is deceptively simple, but making it sound right involves listening to yourself carefully as you practice:

- Be sure to start with your hands meeting as shown on page 21...
- Move your right hand away from your left hand as shown below:

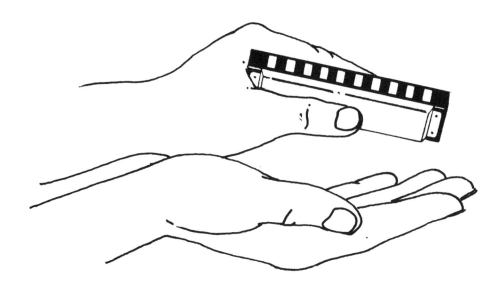

Vibrato

- Move your fingers far apart, but keep your left palm and right wrist close together.

If this method feels a little awkward at first, try imagining a loose-fitting hinge holding your left palm and right wrist close to one another, while allowing your right palm and fingers to move freely (remember not to move your *left* hand).

Now try this vibrato as you play the C scale (4↑ —7↑ on page 13) slowly. Start each note without vibrato, then move your right hand slowly at first and then gradually faster. Your right hand should touch your left lightly, but with some authority, on every vibrato *cycle* (each time your hands separate and move together again). If your hands don't touch or touch too lightly, your vibrato will be faint and indefinite. If your hands are too stiff and touch with too much force, your vibrato will sound harsh ("wa-wa"-like, which is great for country blues but bad for vibrato).

Add vibrato to the long notes of the melodies in the previous chapters, starting each note with a straight tone (no vibrato) and moving your right hand slowly at first and gradually faster. This approach to vibrato is a lot like that of a good singer. (Some people say the harmonica is really sung rather than played.)

In *"Shenandoah,"* pay particular attention to the leaps from hole 4 to hole 6. Practice these separately until they sound as smooth as your playing of adjacent holes. Play this melody with straight tones, then gradually add vibrato, mainly on the longer notes.

Muted Tones

For a new color, try playing with the vibrato-cupping position, but without moving your right hand or left fingers. This will give you a *muted sound* which, when used in combination with open-handed straight tone playing and vibrato, adds a nice contrast between the various sections of *"Shenandoah."*

◆9 Shenandoah

American Traditional

Barbara Allen

A pretty Scottish traditional song…this version is in 3/4 time (3 beats per measure). After the three note pick-up, a light vibrato will sound good, particularly on the longer notes.

Scottish Traditional

Although *"The Streets Of Laredo"* is somewhat mournful, play it at a steady waltz tempo (1, 2, 3, — 1, 2, 3).

This song uses repeat signs and first and second endings which indicate:

- Play the quarter note pick-up, then play bars 1 — 8.
- Repeat bars 1 — 6, skip bars 7 and 8 (the "first ending"), and go to bars 9 and 10 (the "second ending").

The Streets Of Laredo

American Traditional

Wildwood Flower

This tune is in 2/4 time (2 beats per measure), and has some fairly large melodic leaps which should be practiced separately at first. Here's a new note:

American Traditional

24

Stretching Out

In this section you'll learn to play in new keys and in a higher register. Most of the examples on the following pages are fairly easy to play.

Turning Another Key

A "key" tells you what scale you are playing, e.g. *key of C — C scale.* The next few songs are in the key of F. You'll find most of them easier than playing in C. (Not all songs in F can be played on your C harmonica.)

The flat sign (♭) following the treble clef is the *key signature,* which tells you that you are playing in the key of F.

⑩ Swing Low, Sweet Chariot
Key of F

Black Spiritual

Largo
Key of F

Anton Dvorak

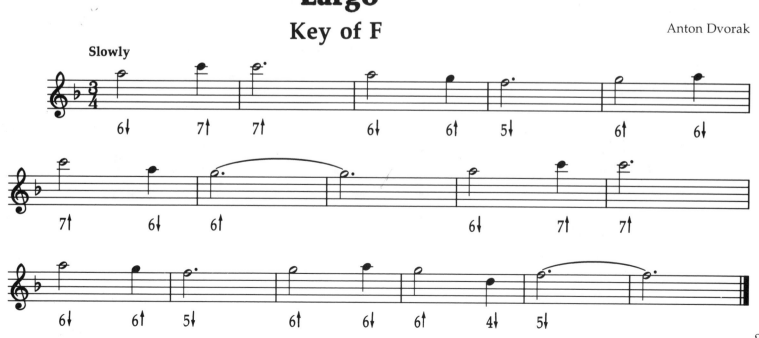

11 Amazing Grace
Key of F

Traditional Gospel

Sixteenth Notes

The next examples introduce you to sixteenth notes:

- Four sixteenth notes equal one quarter note: = 1 beat

- Two sixteenth notes equal one eighth note: = ½ beat

Sixteenth notes are counted as follows:

one - a - & - a - two - a - & - a - three - a - & - a - four - a - & - a

CHALLENGE BOX — 16th Notes: Here's an exercise in counting sixteenth notes as they are most commonly used in the songs you'll be learning:

Practice counting this exercise slowly at first. Steadiness is more important than speed at this point.

Here's a C scale in a higher register. The *8va sign* above the staff indicates that the notes are to be played one octave (8 scale notes) higher than written in music notation.

◆12 See You At High C

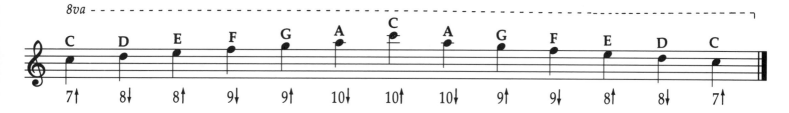

Since the scale is arranged a little differently in this register, a little practice is a good idea. You'll notice that the seventh scale note (B) is missing. Pay particular attention to the fact that, unlike in the lower register, 4↑—7↑, you have to *change holes* in order to move from C/7↑ to D/8↓, E/8↑ to F/9↓, or G/9↑ to A/10↓. However, you *do not* change holes when moving from D/8↓ to E/8↑, or F/9↓ to G/9↑.

Because of the stiffness of the reeds in this register, particularly the draw reeds, you get greater tonal clarity and more accurate pitch if you play these notes more lightly than those on the lower-numbered holes.

Learning songs in more than one key is a good way to expand your ear and improve your technique. Here is *"Wabash Cannonball"* back-to-back in the keys of C and F.

◆13 Wabash Cannonball

Key of C

American Traditional

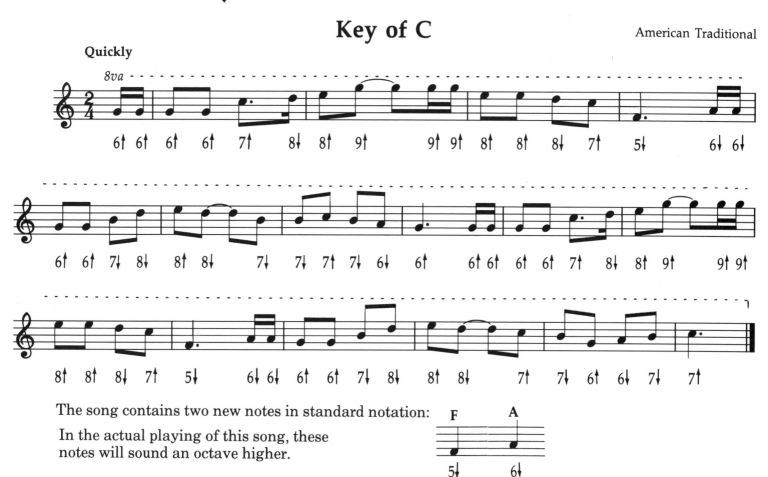

The song contains two new notes in standard notation:

In the actual playing of this song, these notes will sound an octave higher.

Wabash Cannonball
Key of F

American Traditional

Amazing Grace

Key of C

Traditional Gospel

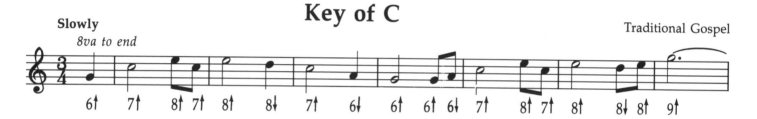

You learned this song in the key of F on page 26. This version involves quite a bit more movement of your harp, since much of the melody is in the upper register.

When you use your right-hand vibrato in this register, you will find that it isn't necessary for your hands to touch when you play the high notes. Experiment by varying the distance between your right hand and left palm.

In the following version of *"Amazing Grace,"* you are playing in G, which is denoted by the sharp symbol (♯) on the first line of the staff. This is the key signature for G major.

Amazing Grace

Key of G

Traditional Gospel

Largo

Key of G

Anton Dvorak

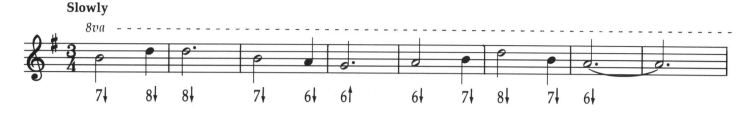

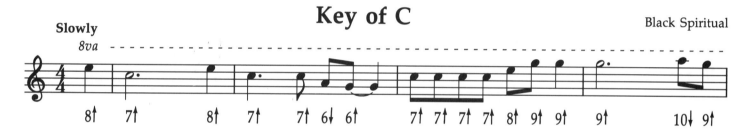

*Because of the use of 8va…, a note is introduced that you have not previously seen in standard notation. This note will sound an octave higher than written:

Swing Low, Sweet Chariot

Key of C

Black Spiritual

Swing Low, Sweet Chariot

Key of G

Black Spiritual

"Little Liza Jane," a traditional folk song, is given here in two keys. Learning this (or any) song back-to-back in two different keys is a great way to train your ear.

◆15 Little Liza Jane in C and G

C Major

G Major

The Yellow Rose Of Texas
Key of C

This song is a good challenging exercise in the upper register, and it will give you practice in playing wide leaps.

Brightly

American Traditional

DISCOGRAPHY

You probably want to hear some outstanding harmonica sounds, so for inspiration and stylization, here's a list of the greats around which you can model your sound.

Carey Bell
Billy Bizor
Sugar Blue
Paul Butterfield
James Cotton
Jesse Fuller
Jazz Gillum
James Harmon Band
Slim Harpo
Big Walter Horton
Howlin' Wolf
Little Walter Jacobs

Magic Dick
Charly Musselwhite
Lee Oskar
Rod Piazza
Jimmy Reed
Corky Siegel
Siegel-Schwall Blues Band
Sonny Terry
Junior Wells
Sonny Boy Williamson
Kim Wilson (Fabulous Thunderbirds)

Stretching Out
A Little Further
Playing In Minor,
or Sounding Sad In One Easy Lesson

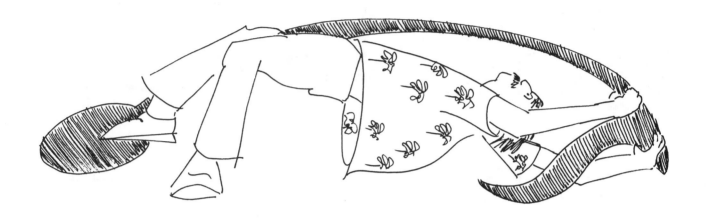

hen you bought your first C harmonica, you may have thought you could only play this instrument in one or two major keys. However, there are three minor keys that you can learn on the C harmonica just as quickly as you learned to play in C.

D Minor

The first of these new keys is D minor.

17 Joshua Fought The Battle Of Jericho

Key of D Minor

On page 25, you learned that a flat sign following the treble clef is the key signature for F major. In minor keys, a single flat is the key signature for D minor.

◆18 Shady Grove
Key of D Minor

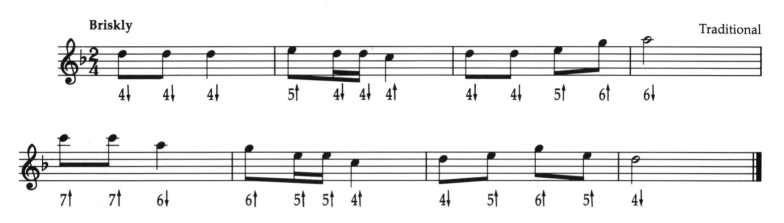

"Scarborough Fair" was part of a 1967 Simon and Garfunkel hit, but actually this melody has been around since the eighteenth century.

Play this song smoothly, with very little "attack" at the beginnings of notes.

Scarborough Fair

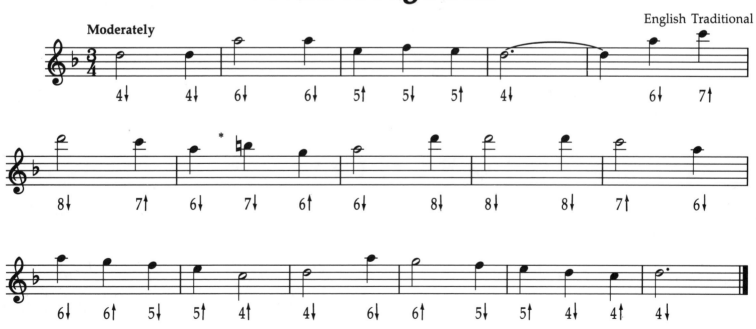

*A natural sign (♮) before the B note cancels the flat. Play this note as a regular B note.

On *"Wayfaring Stranger,"* try using closed hand tones, open-hand dead tones (no vibrato), and hand vibrato. Begin mixing the colors (vibrato, mute, open-hand) in a way that sounds good to you.

⬥19 Wayfaring Stranger
Key of D Minor

Black Spiritual

*A quarter rest indicates *one* beat of silence

A Minor

The next minor key is A minor, which has no sharps or flats in its key signature.

⬥20 All The Pretty Little Horses

Moderately

Traditional Lullabye

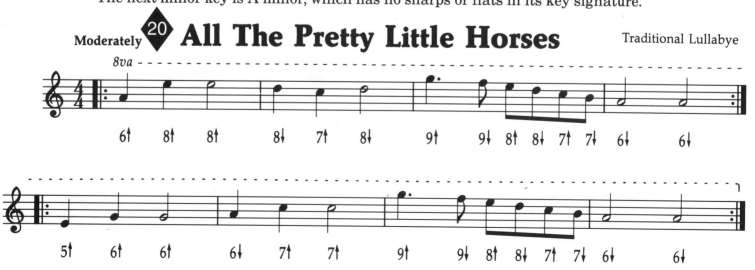

Shady Grove in A Minor

Key of A Minor

Joshua Fought The Battle Of Jericho

Key of A Minor

"When Johnny Comes Marching Home," an up-tempo Civil War era march, is written in 6/8 time: 6 beats in a measure; an eighth note gets one beat. This time signature is easy to master if you think of each measure as containing a pair of threes:

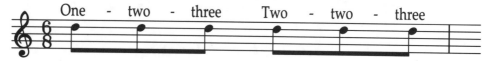

Play it slowly at first, until all the sections are equally smooth. Then, establish a quick march tempo.

When Johnny Comes Marching Home

E Minor

The last minor key you'll learn to play on your harmonica is E minor. The key signature for E minor is one sharp (♯):

• A sharp symbol (♯) indicates that a note is raised by one half-step
• A flat symbol (♭) indicates that a note is lowered by one half-step
• A natural symbol (♮) cancels a sharp or flat previously on that note.

⬧22 Pretty Polly

Mack's Minor Melody

David McKelvy

Take It E'zy

David McKelvy

Part II: PLAYING TECHNIQUES AND STYLES

Bending, Blues, Rock, Country, And Other New Sounds

In the remainder of this book you'll learn a whole new set of playing techniques and styles. These include bending, lipping, throat vibrato and blow bends, along with how they are used to play blues, rock and country music.

Blue Notes, Cross Harp & Bending
(Or Everything That's Old Is New Again)

While the overall sound, instrumentation and arrangements of pop and rock music change from decade to decade, the sounds and styles of popular harmonica players remain remarkably similar to those of the Chicago-style players of the '50s and '60s. Many of the traditional *country blues* styles continue to be heard in country-western arrangements, regardless of the other changes that take place in that idiom. Diatonic harmonica is one of the few instruments on which you are being current by being traditional.

About 95% of the blues, rock and country-western harp playing you'll hear is in cross-harp position. "Cross Harp" means that you are playing in the key that is four notes below the key of your harmonica which, on a C harp, is G (you've already done this).

Plus…you are going to be playing in a style that involves bending, scoops and other stylizations that employ the unique characteristics of this position.

So far, you've covered six different keys on your 10-hole harmonica, and there's a lot more that you can learn. Seek out other examples on your own; listen to recordings, radio, etc. Experiment! Try playing melodies by ear.

In order to master blues, rock and country playing, you'll learn a couple of new techniques — *lipping and bending*.

This is one of the most important chapters in this book, so read it carefully, practice the examples slowly, and enjoy playing!

Lipping

Lipping is the method by which you produce a single note by covering just one hole with your lips, *without using your tongue.* The technique is illustrated here:

In the illustrations you'll notice that:

- Your harmonica is still *in your mouth* (though obviously not to the degree it is in tongue-blocking).
- Your lips are open enough to allow space for one complete hole. Puckering too tightly will result in a loss of volume and tone.
- Your jaw remains relaxed and the inside of your mouth open, just as if you were tongue-blocking. This is very important where tone is concerned. Remember, that the inside of your mouth and throat are part of your total instrument. Without them, your tone tends to be rather thin.

You learn tongue-blocking first because it gives you good tone by forcing you to play with the inside of your mouth open. The object here is for you to get the single notes as clean and open-sounding by lipping as you got by tongue-blocking.

As you experiment with single notes by lipping, you should occasionally play a given note by tongue-blocking *and* lipping, comparing the tones. The more you open the inside of your mouth when you play, the greater your volume will be and the better your tone. If you hear more than one note, try shifting your harmonica slightly; if that doesn't work, narrow your lips just a bit.

"Lipping Blues" introduces you to cross harp blues position in which you are playing in the key of G. This melody uses a note you already know, but on a different reed:

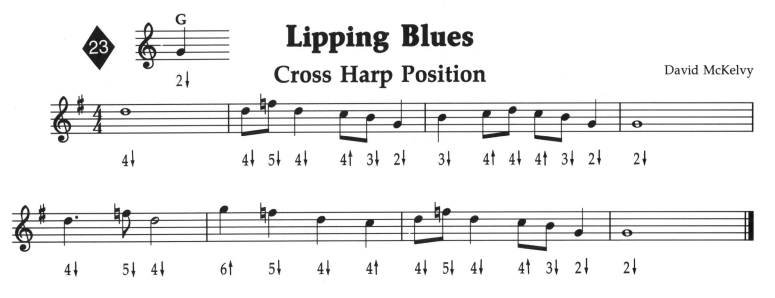

Once you are able to get one note this new way, try playing the scales and tunes you've already learned using single-note lipping.

◆24 Bending

By adding *bending* to your techniques, you will not only be able to play new notes, but you'll also learn to produce the sounds heard in blues, rock and country music.

Bending has two main functions: To play new pitches and to get new sounds (or tones). If you've ever listened to recordings of some of the great blues harmonica players, you may have noticed that they *slide up* to certain pitches. Some players perform these slides very slowly (such as the late Sonny Terry), and provide the best examples for you at this point.

What you do when you bend a note is *to create additional pressure on the reeds of your harp by changing the shape of the inside of your mouth.*

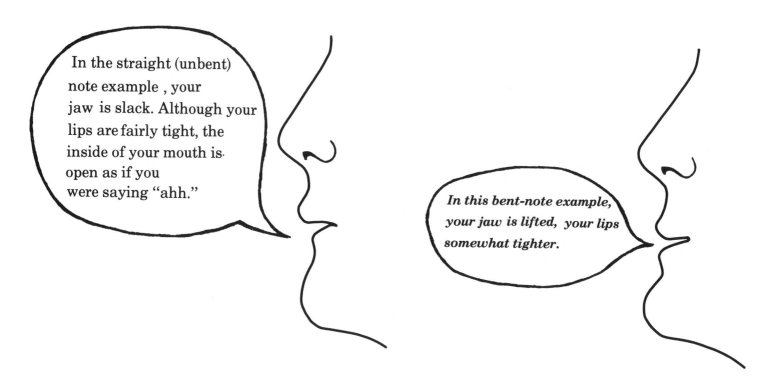

In the straight (unbent) note example , your jaw is slack. Although your lips are fairly tight, the inside of your mouth is open as if you were saying "ahh."

In this bent-note example, your jaw is lifted, your lips somewhat tighter.

The sound of the bent note will be slightly more muted and less "reedy" than your unbent note, but should still be clear and have definite pitch.

4-Draw Bend

The easiest note for most players to bend at first is a 4 draw/D. By bending this reed you are able to play D♭, which is a half-step lower than D. The tablature for this bend is 4 ↲. Here's how:

Begin by playing this note straight, using lipping.

- Lift your jaw slowly and...
- Tighten your lips.
- Lift your tongue towards the roof of your mouth; and...
- Increase the amount of air you inhale. (Eventually this won't be necessary, but for now it can be helpful.)

The sound you will hear is like a slur down from D to D♭. Bending is a little tricky to learn at first, but once you bend your first note, it gets a lot easier (funny how that is!).

As you practice bending 4-draw and the other notes you're about to cover:

- Do not change the angle of your harmonica in your mouth by pushing it down.
- Do not pucker your lips too tightly! This will result in a thin, somewhat "tinny" tone and a loss of volume.

Once you succeed in bending the note lower:

- Practice releasing the bent note *slowly* to the straight (unbent) tone.
- Practice bending 4-draw and releasing your bend *slowly* and then *quickly*. This will help you gain better control of bent notes.
- Practice bending 4↓/D to 4↲/D♭

 # A Foretaste Of 4-Draw Bends In Four
Cross Harp Position

This tune features eighth note *triplets* — a group of three notes performed in the time of two. These are indicated by a "3" at the stem of a note.*

David McKelvy

2-Draw Bend

When you are fairly comfortable bending 4-draw, try applying the same technique to the draw reed of hole number 2/G. Notice that the *placement* or *center* of your tone is deeper in your throat than on hole number 4. This is true of both your unbent and bent notes on 2-draw. In general, higher notes have smaller resonating chambers than lower notes.

Practice bending 2↓/G to 2↲/F. Once again, don't be afraid to draw more air when you first learn to bend the 2-draw reed. Sometimes you'll draw so hard it'll feel like your eyes are going to pop out. Don't worry, once you've bent any given reed a few times, you'll get a feel for bending, and you'll be able to bend notes without inhaling a lot of additional air. Yes, it gets easier! Don't get discouraged!

26 2-Draw Bends In A Four Bar Melody
Cross Harp Position

David McKelvy

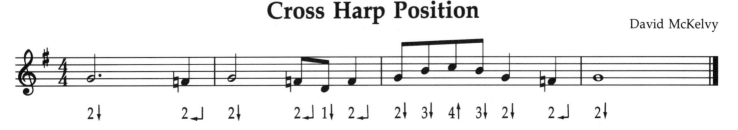

Before attempting to bend the remaining holes, look at the following chart of all the straight and bent notes available on the first six holes of your harmonica.

The tablature sign for a half-bend is, ♪ while ♫ indicates a full bend.

On any given hole, only the higher-pitched reed can be bent down in pitch.

On this chart, you'll notice that only the draw notes bend. You'll also notice that:

- On each hole, your draw note bends *down* to a pitch one half-step higher than the blow note of that same hole and, therefore…

- The draw notes on holes 1, 4, and 6 bend *only one half-step while*…

- 2-draw will bend down *two* half-steps, and 3-draw bends down *three* half-steps.

- 5-draw does not bend down since its pitch (F) is only a half-step above that of 5 blow (E).

*Try bending 2↓/G again, this time bending a half-step to 2♪/F♯ and then a whole step to 2♫/F. Try bending and releasing these notes slowly at first then quickly. Listen to your notes carefully for pitch accuracy.

3-Draw Bend

- Practice bending 3↓/B a half-step to 3♪Bb and releasing your bend.
- Slowly bend 3↓/B a whole step to 3♫/A. Release your bend slowly until you hear 3↓/B once again.
- 3-draw is fairly easy to bend, but tricky to control. Avoid over-bending to 3↘/Ab .

1-Draw Bend

- Practice bending 1↓/D to 1♫/Db. The placement of both the bent and unbent pitches on 1-draw should be deeper in your throat than on the other notes.

6-Draw Bend

- The remaining bendable draw note is 6↓/A which bends to 6♫/Ab. Since the placement of the notes on 6-draw is a little shallower in your throat, practice bending this note with a tighter, slightly closed-mouth position.

As you practice bending notes, particularly your lower-pitched reeds, you'll gradually get a deeper, richer tone, which will help you become a "bluesier" sounding player.

Sometimes blues, rock and country musicians refer to a short series of notes as a *lick*. A lick is used to fill short spaces between vocal lines or as part of a lead solo line.

◆28 Blues Licks Using 2, 3 and 4 Bends

Cross Harp Position

"*Scaling The Blues*" is in 12/8 time, a common time signature in rock and blues: 12 beats in a measure; an eighth note gets one beat. Both bars of this exercise should be played as four sets of loose-feeling triplets. The main purpose of the piece is to give you the ability to play bent notes from hole to hole without an audible break.

Practice this example very slowly and out of tempo at first, until it sounds completely smooth. Then gradually build your tempo.

◆29 Scaling The Blues

"*David's Country Blues*" uses a lot of bending on holes 2, 3 and 4. The "wa" sign that you see over some of the notes indicates a particular inflection: You "scoop" up to your note by bending very slightly and releasing your bend very quickly. You can also begin with a closed-hand position and open your right hand (or left fingers) just as you release your bend.

It won't take much practice to learn to coordinate these skills, but be careful! Use this technique sparingly; *too many* "wa's" (or scoops) detract from the melody you are playing and give your overall sound a certain choppiness. Keep it lean and keep it clean.

43

30 David's Country Blues
Cross Harp Position

David McKelvy

In this and other songs that follow, chord symbols are added to the music. These will help other musicians, especially keyboard and guitar players, to accompany you or improvise. For an explanation of how chords are used specifically in blues, turn to *Playing With Other Pickers* (page 63) in the *"Bonus"* section.

The examples here are written rhythmically "straighter" than they should actually be performed. If you listen to recordings of blues harp artists, you'll notice a looseness of phrasing that gives the blues its feel. The combinations of licks, riffs and lines that go into creating a solo are limitless. The following examples will get you started. Learn them straight at first, note-by-note, and loosen them up.

31 Country Blues Shuffle
Cross Harp Position

David McKelvy

12 Bar Blues Shuffle
Cross Harp Position

Medium tempo

David McKelvy

CHALLENGE BOX — Rests: Rests are beats on which no note is played. The types of rests are:

Whole rest:		= 4 beats of silence
Half rest:		= 2 beats of silence
Quarter rest:		= 1 beat of silence
Eighth rest:		= ½ beat of silence
Sixteenth rest:		= ¼ beat of silence

A New Sound—The Throat Vibrato

Those of you who took up harmonica in order to learn blues and rock playing were probably inspired by the special and unique sounds of at least one of the well-known players. Whether you heard your blues harp idols on record or in concert, you always went away wishing you could play like them.

The special sounds of most famous players involve both phrasing and tone. In playing blues and rock harmonica styles, your tone is in your throat, and that tone is colored by the tasteful use of the throat vibrato. Of all the famous rock, country and blues harpists, no two sound exactly alike, just as no two singers sound alike. But all great players have certain techniques in common.

In order to get a clear-sounding throat vibrato, do the following:
- Place your harmonica in your mouth in a lipping position over hole 2.
- Tighten your lips and lift your jaw very slightly.
- Exhale a quick burst of air, as if you were coughing very lightly.
- From the same part of your throat in which you exhaled, inhale once very quickly and then stop.
- Inhale again very quickly and then several times in succession at a steady rate

What you should hear at this point is a series of short-sounding notes, but as you soften the edge in your throat, you'll notice your short notes blending into a single note with vibrato:

Try the same technique on holes 1, 3, and 4. (5-draw is not quite as good for vibrato, since it can't bend down fully, and bendable notes are better for vibrato.) If you have a lower-key harp (e.g., G or A), try your vibrato on 6-draw. Eventually you'll be able to get a 6-draw vibrato on your C harp, but for now stick to the lower holes.

Getting a good steady throat vibrato will take some time, but with a lot of practice you'll learn it. The new blues sound you'll get will be worth all the effort.

As you practice throat vibrato, make sure that…

- You are not moving your tongue. (Sometimes beginning players will do this to "assist" their vibratos, but it never sounds right and only gets in the way.)

- You are not using your hand vibrato at the same time you are practicing throat vibrato. The sounds just don't mix.

- The speed of your vibrato is steady.

- Your lips and jaw don't get too tight. Stay relaxed. Remember that the positions of your lips and jaw are only slightly more closed in vibrato position than in straight-tone position. Tightening your lips and jaw *very slightly* helps create a back pressure on the reeds, which, in turn, gives your tone the right placement in your throat.

At first, practice vibrato separately on your melodies where vibrato fits best. Think of yourself singing (yes, your harp is a singing instrument!). Choose where and when to use vibrato in the same way a singer would. Long notes are generally best; start your note with a straight tone and let your vibrato build.

Once again, learning how to play and use throat vibrato won't happen overnight, but keep practicing and review all the instructions in this section from time to time. Listen to your favorite blues harp players for inspiration.

Many of the cross harp melodies you've already learned sound great with throat vibrato. Turn back to page 39 and take another look at *"Lipping Blues."* Since the melody is played slowly, many of the long notes are excellent for practicing your vibrato, particularly the sustained 4↓/D in the first measure, and the whole notes 2↓/G in the fourth and eighth measures.

Similarly, *"A Foretaste of 4-Draw Bends in Four Bars,"* will give you a good workout with vibrato on holes 2 and 4, this time at a more challenging (medium) tempo. Practice until you can perform your vibrato on the longer notes without sounding choppy. Your throat tone and vibrato will only add to the overall sound of a song if there is no break in the tempo. Practice *"Long Note Blues"* until the long notes with vibrato blend with the other parts of the melody.

◆33 Long Note Blues
Cross Harp Position

A Taste Of Other Blues Positions

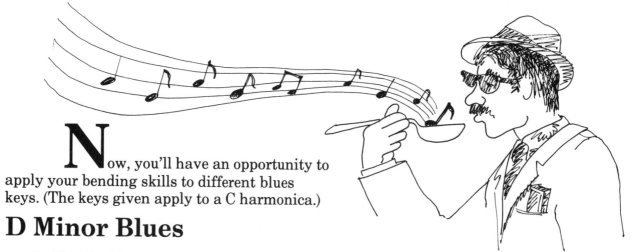

Now, you'll have an opportunity to apply your bending skills to different blues keys. (The keys given apply to a C harmonica.)

D Minor Blues

In *"It's De Minor Blues,"* you are applying your blues-bending technique in the key of D minor. This is sometimes referred to as "third position" blues.

◆34 It's De Minor Blues

This 8-bar tune is played with a shuffle feel.

David McKelvy

On page 34, you learned a "straight" version of *"Wayfaring Stranger."* Here it is with added bends and scoops ("wa's") and different phrasing to give it a bluesy, gospel feel. Play it slowly and out of tempo, with very little vibrato. Use the colors of your bent notes to give the passages your own flavor.

When you scoop up to a bent note ("wa"), do it quickly, and make sure your release from the bent note is complete.

◆35 Wayfaring Stranger

Blues, Gospel Style   Key of D Minor

Black Spiritual

Playing Blues In E Minor

E Minor Blues Scale

This scale involves two bends -2 ♪/F♯, and 3↲/A. Because of the bluesy "bent" sound of this register, E minor sounds a lot funkier here than in the upper register version on page 37. This blues scale is sometimes referred to as "fourth position" blues.

Guitarist's Favorite Blues in E Minor

Getting A Few More Notes

Blow Bends

In the *Blue Notes, Cross Harp And Bending* section, you learned that:

- On any given hole only your higher-pitched reed can be bent down in pitch and…
- The bendable reed can be bent down to a half-step above the lower-pitched reed.

In the upper register (holes 8 through 10), your higher-pitched reeds are on your blow notes. The blow bends in this register are illustrated here.

As you look at the chart:

- Notice that 8 blow and 9 blow can be bent down a half-step (8↑/E to 8↿/E♭, and 9↑/G to 9↿/G♭, respectively)…

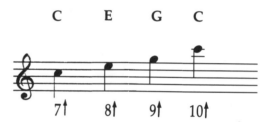

 37

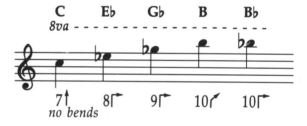

- While 10 blow can be bent down two half-steps (10↑/C to either 10↿/B, or 10↿/B♭). Since the notes on hole 7 are only a half-step apart, 7↓/B and 7↑/C, neither note is bendable.

The technique for bending blow notes is essentially the same as for bending draw reed notes: You increase the pressure on a reed by narrowing the passage of air through your mouth to a *very tight* closed ("oo" sound) position. Your cheeks and lips should be particularly tight.

Since higher-pitched reeds can be tricky to bend, this might be a good time to buy a lower-pitched harmonica (G or A) in order to make practicing these bends a little easier. Playing different keyed harps is also good for your ear, and will enable you to play with other musicians in *their* various keys.

◆ **38** **High Note Blues**

David McKelvy

Key of C

Practice Those Blow Bends

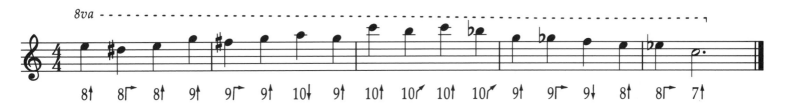

◆39 Straight Ahead Blues

Key of C

Slow shuffle

David McKelvy

*An eighth rest indicates one-half beat of silence.

Playing Two Or Three Holes At A Time

You can play two adjacent notes at a time from either tongue-blocking or lipping positions. From your tongue-blocking, simply move your tongue slightly to the left until you hear two clear notes. Two notes played at one time are referred to as "double stops."

In order to get a double stop from your lipping position, you expand your lips until you hear your second note as clearly as your first. (For playing three or four notes at a time, use lipping.)

Try the following version of *"Red River Valley"* using tongue-blocking and then lipping. In this version, wherever there are two notes played simultaneously, the lower note is the melody. Practice the melody line first, then add the harmony notes:

 Red River Valley

Traditional

 Tongue Splitting

Tongue-splitting is an extremely useful technique in all styles — from blues to bluegrass — as well as all major and minor keys.

Tongue splitting simply means using tongue-blocking in order to get notes from both the right and left sides of your mouth, while covering the middle holes, as illustrated here:

You'll notice that in the two diagrams, different numbers of holes are blocked by your tongue. For the first time in your playing, it will be necessary for you to cover a precise number of holes with both your lips and tongue.

When you first attempt this technique, it may feel like learning tongue-blocking all over again, but the end result will be worth the effort.

◆42 Octaves

Practice the following exercise in which you play notes that are an octave apart from one another:

Octaves

Root-Seven Split

This split is used quite a bit by blues and country harp players. The sound is funky and adds a lot to your playing, whether you are accompanying other players or taking a solo. It's played like this:

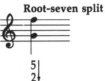

Once you are comfortable with this split, you can even add a slight trembling sound by quickly fluttering the back part of your tongue while keeping the front of your tongue over holes 3 and 4.

In *"Snake Tongue Blues"* practice the melody, which is in the upper line, first:

◆43 Snake Tongue Blues
Cross Harp Position

David McKelvy

Tongue Rhythms

Sometimes the solos, riffs and fills used by the better blues, rock and country artists involve playing more than one note at a time; some passages have rhythmic punches with *chords* (groups of three or more notes played at one time).

While no two players approach chord rhythms in exactly the same way, the methods that follow will help you master the basic principles and techniques that all good chord playing has in common.

Fullness Of Tone

When you begin practicing chords and chord rhythms, a good clear tone is still the most important thing. Your rhythms should punctuate, but never break up the sound you're getting from your harmonica.

When you play tongue rhythms, you should begin with an open "ah" sound. As you lift your tongue quickly, your vowel sound will change to a short "i" sound ("i" as in "it") just before you tap your tongue on the roof of your mouth. Tap lightly! It doesn't take much to get the point across.

The tablature for groups of notes used in tongue rhythms looks like this:

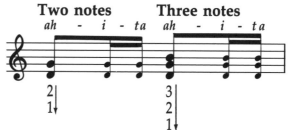

Remember to tap your tongue lightly and release it quickly. If you tap too hard, or hold your tongue close to the roof of your mouth for too long after your tongue-tap, your chords will sound choppy and you'll lose tone. Relax.

44 The Rhythmic Tongue

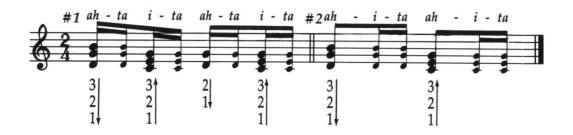

Boil That Cabbage Down
Cross Harp Position

Lively   American Traditional

Trills, Shakes and Tremolos

In blues harp playing, all these terms refer to the same thing: You move your harp rapidly back and forth between two holes. The effect you get from this motion is colorful and useful in country, as well as blues playing. In cross harp playing, the most useful "shakes" are between holes 4 and 5, and holes 3 and 4.

The tablature and notation used here for a shake are:

There are two common ways of getting a two-hole shake—by moving your harmonica with your right hand, and by shaking your head slightly from left to right.

The Hand Shake (More Than A Friendly Gesture)

In order to get a good steady right hand shake, lighten your left hand grip. Use your right thumb and index finger to shake your harmonica left and right slowly, so that you hear each of your two trilled notes clearly. When you become comfortable doing this, gradually shake your harp a little faster.

Since a shake will only sound good if it's well-controlled, make sure that each note is equally loud and clear, no matter how fast you shake your harp. Always limit the width of your shake, so that you never hear more than the two intended notes.

The right-handed method for shaking (or trilling) notes sounds okay in some country and country blues styles, but in order to get a real funky sounding shake — one that will sound good when played through an amp — you should learn the method that involves moving your head.

The Head Shake

The head shake might seem a little funny, since all your playing up to this point has involved holding your head still and moving your harp. But actually learning to shake (or trill) with either your hand or head will be easier than many of the techniques you've already learned. As with a lot of things that come easily, shakes are often overdone. Just remember that less is more! Pick those parts of your solos where shaking actually adds something to the music.

To learn this technique:
- Begin by shifting your head slightly to the right until you hear a new note,
- Then shift back to the left until you hear your original note clearly.
- Repeat this procedure, gradually increasing the speed until you can produce a good clean blend of the two notes.

When using a head shake, *hold your hands still.*

 # Anticipation Blues
Cross Harp Position

David McKelvy

Slow shuffle

By now, hopefully you've begun playing along with people who play other instruments and even with recordings! Listen to recordings of the great blues, country and rock players for examples of how to enhance your playing. Be aware that each instrument has a role in making the overall sound work.

This book provides you with the techniques for learning all the notes on your harp, but the experience of listening and playing will gradually teach you how to use your knowledge of notes and the "licks" to become a musician. Best of luck to all of you! Listen, play and enjoy.

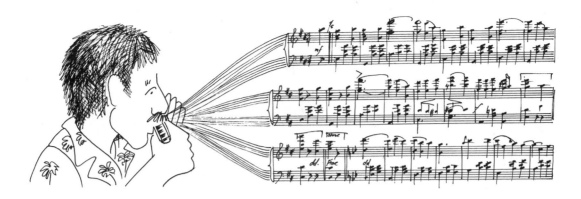

DAVID'S BONUS SECTION

Congratulations! By learning the techniques and music in this book, you have mastered all the basics you'll need to eventually play in any style you choose — blues, rock, country, traditional. For both practice and plain fun, here are some more songs to play. All of the techniques for playing them are covered in the book.

Amazing Grace
Cross Harp Position

When The Saints Go Marching In
Cross Harp Position

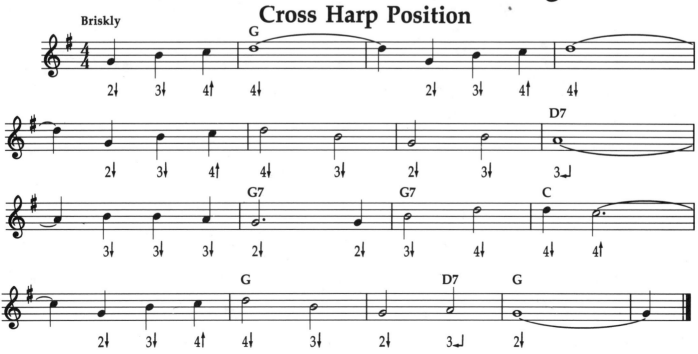

Ode To Joy

Key of C
Tongue Splitting

Ludwig Van Beethoven

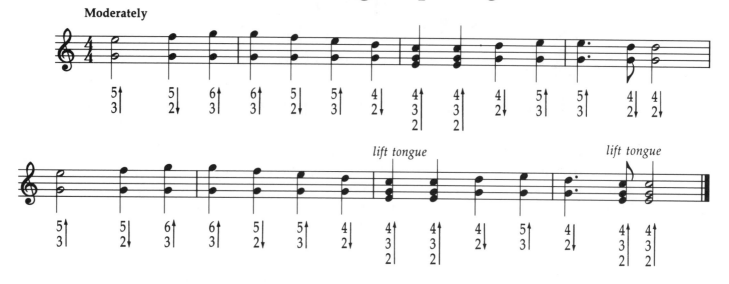

49 ◆ Old Joe Clark

Key of G

Traditional

Tongue Splitting

◇50 **Drunken Sailor**
Key of D Minor

Sea Chanty

Tongue lifting is a fairly easy and interesting technique used for rhythmic self-accompaniment. Here's how you do it: Using tongue blocking, you simply lift your tongue on and off of the holes to your left, while carrying the melody on the right side of your mouth.

Wildwood Flower

American Traditional

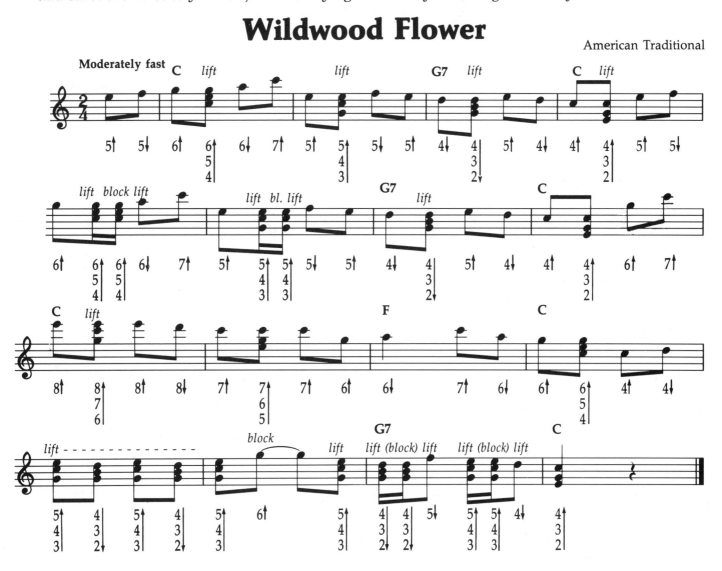

51 ◆ Star Of County Down
Key of A Minor

"Star of County Down" is one of my all-time favorite melodies. Since much of the beauty of this song is harmonic, find someone to play along with you, especially on guitar or keyboard. Play this tenderly at a slow waltz tempo.

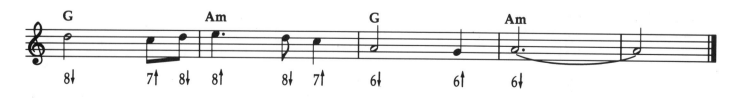

◆52◆ Arkansas Traveler

American Traditional

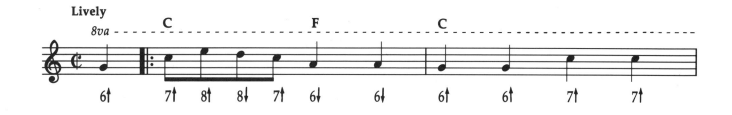

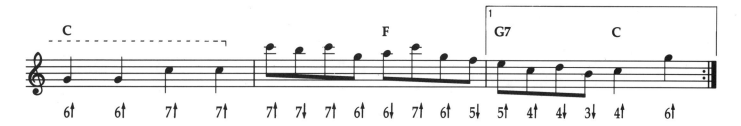

◆53 Zig Zag Jig
Key of C
Wide Leaps
Try this one unaccompanied.

Irish Traditional

Playing With Other "Pickers"

As you listen to songs on your favorite blues harmonica albums, begin focusing on the background tracks. The bass and drums are playing the rhythms, and the guitar and/or keyboards not only reinforce these rhythms, but also play the chord accompaniment to the harmonica solos.

- A *chord* is a group of three or more notes played simultaneously.
- A *progression* is a sequence of chords used to *accompany* a melody.

Chords have numbers as well as names. These numbers are assigned according to where the chords begin in the scale:

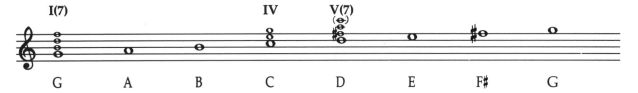

For example, in the key of G:
- G is the first note, therefore a G chord is the I chord.
- C is the fourth note of the scale, making the C chord a IV chord.
- D is the fifth note of the scale, making the D chord a V chord.

When you play harmonicas in different keys, the names of the chords change but the numbers (I, IV, V) remain the same, since they describe the relationship between the chords and the key in which you're playing.

There are many blues that have a standard "blues progression." For instance, the progression (sequence) of chords in *"David's Country Blues"* (key of G) goes like this:

Measures 1-3 ..... are accompanied by a G (I) chord,
Measure 4 .... is accompanied G^7 (I^7) chord,
Measures 5-6 ..... are accompanied by a C (IV) chord,
Measures 7-8 ..... are accompanied by another G (I) chord,
Measure 9 .... is accompanied by a D^7 (V^7) chord,
Measure 10 .... is accompanied by another C (IV) chord,
Measures 11-12 ... are accompanied by a G (I) chord.
    (if this sequence of chords is to be repeated, a D^7 would
    accompany the last half of the 12th measure)

Because of the numerical relationship between the chords in this sequence, this progression is sometimes called a *one-four-five* (I-IV-V) progression.

Learning to play with blues progressions is important. Once you know a lot of licks, you need to know where those licks should be played.

David's Country Blues
Cross Harp Position

David McKelvy

Harmonicas Used In Different Playing Positions

The following table is useful for finding the major and minor keys that can be played on harmonicas tuned in keys other than C major.

All the keys can be found on the table according to their position on the C harmonica. For example, on a G harmonica you are playing in D minor position and want to know in what key you are: Find "G" in the *"Harmonica"* column, and move right to the *"D Minor Position"* column. You'll find that you are playing in A minor.

If you want to play in the key of G minor and prefer using the D minor playing position, you'll need to find the key of the harmonica to use: Look down the *"D Minor Position"* column until you find G minor. Then look left to the *"Harmonica"* column where you'll find F for the harmonica you'll need to play.

Harmonica	C Position	G or Cross Position	F Position	D Minor Position	E Minor Position	A or Pure Minor Position
C	C major	G major	F major	D minor	E minor	A minor
G	G major	D major	C major	A minor	B minor	E minor
D	D major	A major	G major	E minor	F♯ minor	B minor
A	A major	E major	D major	B minor	C♯ minor	F♯ minor
E	E major	B major	A major	F♯ minor	A♭ minor	D♭ minor
B	B major	F♯ major	E major	D♭ minor	E♭ minor	A♭ minor
F♯	F♯ major	C♯ major	B major	A♭ minor	B♭ minor	E♭ minor
D♭	D♭ major	A♭ major	F♯ major	E♭ minor	F minor	B♭ minor
A♭	A♭ major	E♭ major	D♭ major	B♭ minor	C minor	F minor
E♭	E♭ major	B♭ major	A♭ major	F minor	G minor	C minor
B♭	B♭ major	F major	E♭ major	C minor	D minor	G minor
F	F major	C major	B♭ major	G minor	A minor	D minor